Davy Crockett

A Captivating Guide to the American Folk Hero Who Fought in the War of 1812 and the Texas Revolution

Free Bonus from Captivating History (Available for a Limited time)

Hi History Lovers!

Now you have a chance to join our exclusive history list so you can get your first history ebook for free as well as discounts and a potential to get more history books for free! Simply visit the link below to join.

Captivatinghistory.com/ebook

Also, make sure to follow us on Facebook, Twitter and Youtube by searching for Captivating History.

Contents

FREE BONUS FROM CAPTIVATING HISTORY (AVAILABLE FOR A LIMITED TIME) 1

INTRODUCTION 3

CHAPTER 1 – THE FRONTIERSMAN 6

CHAPTER 2 – THE MILITIAMAN 12

CHAPTER 3 – THE CONGRESSMAN 17

CHAPTER 4 – THE CELEBRITY 25

CHAPTER 5 – GONE TO TEXAS: THE FREEDOM FIGHTER 29

CHAPTER 6 – THE MYTH 39

REFERENCES 42

Introduction

If, as historian Thomas Carlyle said, the history of the world is but the biography of great men, then it is also true that the story of the great men is a parable of their times, places, and generational aspirations. The life of Davy Crockett, one of the most cherished and remembered American frontiersmen, is an accurate representation of the United States as it stretched westward to become one of the largest nations in the world.

Yet David Crockett was not a mythical character but a very real person. Such was his mark in the process of westward expansion that, among hundreds of other frontiersmen, only he got the informal title of "King of the Wild Frontier" for posterity. The frontiersmen were a special class of rambling men, explorers, naturalists, hunters, and pioneers who formed the vanguard in the territories beyond the Mississippi. As such, they were the eyes and ears of a nation that was craving more territory, excited by the promise of a safe route to the Pacific. But America was not discovered by the Europeans. When the British and French arrived, the native peoples had been living on the continent for centuries. So, the westward expansion was also inevitably the story of the struggle between whites and Native Americans.

Davy Crockett represented the best of that generation because, although he took part in the wars against the Native Americans, when he was a congressman in Washington, he vehemently opposed the land dispossession and injustices against the Native Americans. Hence a long political rivalry arose between the ill-tempered President Andrew Jackson and the silver-tongued adventurer. Crockett did not earn a place in Congress for his noble birth or political patronage. In fact, he was one of the first examples of a genuine man of humble extraction reaching such a high political position. Crockett had spent his childhood with a family burdened by debt and had to work before reaching adolescence to help his father pay it off. His success as a politician was helped in no small measure by his extraordinary eloquence, which made him famous, and the tales of his incredible adventures in the wild that circulated in his lifetime. During a good part of his existence, he made a living as a bear hunter in the Tennessee forests, selling the fur, oil, and meat of the animals. We can say with certainty that Davy Crockett was a tough, hardened, and skilled man, with a deep understanding of the natural world.

When he was alive, books about his adventures, unauthorized biographies, almanacs, and even plays—think of them as the equivalent of the great movie premieres of our times—were produced lavishly, in some cases with such crazy stories that Crockett himself was compelled to write his own books to correct the inaccuracies. Crockett also wrote because, although he was far from being a literary genius or a great naturalist, he was moved by a spirit of openness to new experiences and new conquests. The fame of this simple American "kid" from Tennessee became even greater decades after his death, to the point of Crockett becoming an undeclared national hero and a symbol of the struggle for freedom. Crockett, of course, owed his greatest boost to fame to the Alamo, an old mission built by the Spanish, where one of the most iconic battles was fought in the Texas War of Independence. Crockett's death among the Alamo's defenders, to whom United States history assigned a special status as martyrs of liberty, elevated him to unsuspected heights. More than one hundred years after his death, he was a superstar and a model for children, who watched his adventures on television. In a way, Crockett was perhaps the first superhero in the history of the United States, although this happened many years after his death in the war against Mexico.

This does not mean that his life was not riddled with controversy or that his true achievements do not continue to be the subject of discussion between historians and laymen. Davy Crockett was a celebrity in life, but he was far from being acknowledged as a national hero. He had many enemies, critics, and detractors who, from the moment he entered politics, tried to ruin and discredit him. People from his homeland of Tennessee came to consider him a traitor because he sided with the Native Americans on delicate issues. Many malicious newspapers accused him of being a compulsive gambler and criticized his drinking escapades. Other questions are raised after reading any "Life" of Crockett: Did he defend the Native Americans for reasons of humanitarianism or just to make life difficult for his political opponents? What was he doing in Texas? Did he go with a political nose in search of power, to rebuild his life, or to help the cause of independence? Did he really die as a hero in the Alamo?

What is undeniable is that Davy Crockett was always faithful to his convictions, as he was guided by a deep commitment to justice, and above all, he was someone who always did what he thought was right, even running to aid his strongest political enemy, President Andrew Jackson, when someone tried to assassinate him. And that philosophy of life—doing the right thing no matter what—is much more than can be said of many others of his generation. That is why David Crockett is one of the great national symbols of the United States of America.

Chapter 1 – The Frontiersman

"Like many of them, I stood no chance to become great in any other way than by accident."
—Davy Crockett

David Crockett was not born in a privileged home. His arrival in this world was on August 17th, 1786, in Tennessee, when the region was still part of North Carolina. He was the fifth of nine children. His father, the son of an Irish couple, was John Wesley Crockett, a veteran of the American Revolution who fought at the Battle of Kings Mountain. After that, he had managed to acquire a piece of land to build a humble log cabin for his family. But beyond that, he hadn't accomplished much more in life except living in debt. Since he was very poor, young David and his brothers grew up without an education, spending most of their lives in the wilderness, where life was hard and every man had to hunt. When Mr. Crockett found someone as poor as he was to start a business in partnership, he invested his few savings in a grist mill, but a sudden flood wiped away his plans to earn a steady income. Years later, Davy wrote about that misfortune in his memoirs, the first of many that would haunt his family: "I remember the water rose so high that it got up into the house we lived in, and my father moved us out of it to keep us from being drowned. I was now about seven or eight years old, and have a pretty distinct recollection of everything that was going on."

After the flood, the senior Crockett moved his family to Jefferson County, where, in 1796, he built a log tavern, which he used to offer lodging and food for travelers between Virginia and Tennessee. The cabin survived until the Civil War, during which it was used as a hospital, and later on, it became a hospice for smallpox patients. Davy's father's tavern "was on a small scale, as he was poor; and the principal accommodations which he kept were for the wagoners who traveled the road." At the same time, Mr. Crockett taught Davy how to shoot a rifle to become a skilled hunter and thus contribute to help put food on the table. Davy's first rifle was called "Betsy," and this firearm is still kept in a museum to this day.

Mr. Crockett's fifth son spent his early years away from school and working for the family, at a time when children were expected to help their parents. He also spent many hours exploring the forests. In the tavern, his first informal school, as these were places where travelers gathered to tell stories, the boy must have heard tales about distant lands that aroused his curiosity. When his father finally sent him to the local school, his stay was short, lasting exactly four days.

In the first week, Davy was the victim of the school's bully—a boy much taller and older than he—and being a self-sufficient person from a young age, he decided to put things right. He waited for the older kid on the road, hidden in the bushes, and when the boy passed by, he jumped like a tiger and beat him up. "I scratched his face all to a flitter jig and soon made him cry for quarters in god earnest." Since he feared the teacher's punishment, or possibly the bully's revenge, Davy decided to stay away from the classroom. Of course, he did not tell this to his parents. What he did was leave home in the morning with his brothers, and before reaching the school, he would sneak out into the woods to explore. He stayed there until it was time to go home. That was how things worked until the principal wrote a letter to his father asking why Davy had stopped going to class. The scolding was so severe that the young man, barely thirteen, decided to run away from home and live on his own.

For the next three years, Davy wandered from town to town, performing several jobs as a hired hand. Finally, at the age of sixteen, he decided he had had enough and returned home. His parents hardly recognized him.

* * *

"Though he was poor, he was an honest man," wrote David Crockett about his old man in his autobiography. David's humble background and the fact that his father spent his life chased by debtors, as well as the constant changes of residence, left a deep mark on his personality. Always wandering from place to place in search of a definite home and never settling permanently in a single place, Davy would always be in search of greener pastures in the pursuance of a fortune that never came. When he was a congressman, he always had the less fortunate in mind. At the start of the westward expansion from the initial colonies on the Atlantic, people who lived bordering the Native American country did so with a feeling of inferiority. They were second-class Americans compared to the urban classes of the East Coast cities. Thus, when Davy became famous, he was truly a "man of the people."

But perhaps money was not the biggest problem for the adolescent Crockett, who felt that he was unlucky in love and he had the idea that he was going to stay alone for the rest of his life. During a hunting expedition, he arrived at the home of a German family, where he spent the night. There he met a girl who seemed to him "as ugly as a stone fence." When she realized that she would not have a chance, she assured her guest that there were plenty of fish in the sea waiting for a good man and promised that she would introduce him to the most beautiful woman his eyes had ever seen if he only attended the "reaping," or harvest celebration. Since it was an opportunity to socialize, drink, tell adventures, and listen to other exaggerated tales, all activities that he enjoyed, Davy agreed. There he met a girl named Polly, whom he liked immediately.

Davy offered his employer, an old Quaker who was his neighbor, a deal, where he would work for six months in exchange for a horse, the first he would ever own and something he saw as necessary to woo the beautiful Polly. However, Polly's mother was not thrilled with the idea of giving her daughter's hand to a nineteen-year-old adventurer who didn't have a penny in his pocket. The girl's father viewed Davy with more sympathy, but the young man knew that without Polly's mother's consent, things would be complicated. One night, Davy was hunting a wolf in a part of the forest that he didn't know, which was very uninhabited, and he lost his way. He was thinking about how he would return home when he suddenly saw "a little woman streaking it along the woods like all wrath." Intrigued, he ran to catch up, determined not to lose sight of her. When he grabbed her, he was surprised to see that it was Polly, who had also gotten lost looking for her father's horses. "She looked sweeter than sugar," wrote Davy, "and by this time I loved her almost well enough to eat her."

Tired of the mother's disdain, Davy asked Polly whether she would agree to go with him if he went to her house with two horses. The young woman nodded. On his way back home, Davy went to see a justice of the peace to get a marriage license. On the fixed day, he rode to the girl's house escorted by a group of relatives, as was the custom in those days. Outside Polly's family's property, he asked Polly if she would marry him and showed her the extra horse. Polly said yes, and they were about to ride off together, but at the last moment, the tearful father stopped Davy and asked him to please have the wedding at his house. Crockett, who had nothing against the old man, told him that he would if Polly's mother asked him too and apologized for the cold shoulder she had given him. The wedding was then held at the girl's house.

The couple was in love, but they were both poor. Davy rented a farm, which had two cows and some calves that Polly's parents had given them as a dowry. Polly also had a sewing wheel, and "she was good at that, and at almost anything else that a woman could do." Despite the fact that the two worked hard, with the arrival of two children, Davy knew that he would have to do something else if he did not want them to starve. The couple left the rental property and settled in Lincoln County near Elk River, an area that was just beginning to become populated. It was there that Davy began to stand out as a hunter. Dissatisfied with the declining population of bears, they moved back to Franklin County, most likely to Polly's chagrin since she saw that nothing of what her husband began bore fruit and since she also had to endure his constant absences. Davy was a restless soul, and apparently, he did not do much for the physical improvement of his house. His passion was in the great outdoors. In the words of Michael Wallis, his most important modern biographer, "Hunting always proved to be Crockett´s salvation, sanctuary, and escape."

For a long time, David lived like a wandering soul, taking his family from one place to another. In every new site that he encountered, he explored, hunted bears with his pack of wild dogs, and sold meat, fur, and fat. When the population of these animals began to decline and new colonists began to push the border farther east, he took his belongings and went in search of more deserted lands, as if he was engaged in an endless search for the right place. Many others like him formed a slow exodus to the west, poor men and their families, burdened with debt, looking for a new beginning. "The frontier was moving on, and David, at the age of twenty-five, wanted to move right along with it," writes Wallis. "As was always his way, he had a desire to know what waited for him on the other side of every river and mountain he encountered. His curiosity and restlessness never wavered."

In 1898, pastor and historian John Cabot Abbott, who also wrote the biographies of Napoleon Bonaparte and Frederick the Great, published his biography of David Crockett and described with great detail this part of his life as a frontiersman.

He loved to wander in busy idleness all the day, with fishing-rod and rifle; and he would often return at night with a very ample supply of game. He would then lounge about his hut, tanning deer skins for moccasins and breeches, performing other little jobs, and entirely neglecting all endeavors to improve his farm, or to add to the appearance or comfort of the miserable shanty which he called his home. In hunting, his skill became very remarkable, and few, even of the best marksmen, could throw the bullet with more unerring aim.

As a skilled hunter and trapper, he traveled around the Mississippi Valley as a fur trader and became acquainted with the Native Americans and their way of life. Perhaps he was curious about these inhabitants and made friends among them, but he was not the only one—a tide of people and speculators penetrating the indigenous country came behind him, and it would not be too long before conflicts exploded.

Chapter 2 – The Militiaman

At the beginning of the 1810s, the conflict between the Native Americans and the white population reached a boiling point as the Anglo-American settlers began to cross the Mississippi to take lands where several native peoples lived. With the number of white settlers and traveling traders rising, a Shawnee leader called Tecumseh and his brother, Lalawethika, better known as the Prophet, began a movement to repel the settlers in the Northwest Territory (modern-day Ohio, Indiana, Illinois, Michigan, Wisconsin, and the northeastern part of Minnesota). The idea was to establish a large confederation that would unite all the Native Americans.

Tecumseh is an important figure in the history of indigenous resistance in America. The occurrence of a series of devastating earthquakes in the central United States just a month after a disgruntled Tecumseh, in the absence of indigenous unity, said he would return home to "stomp the ground," convinced many that the Great Spirit was with him and that the time had come to push the whites out of their ancestors' lands. "Your blood is white! You do not believe the Great Spirit sent me. You shall believe it. I will leave directly and go straight to Detroit. When I get there, I will stamp my foot on the ground and shake down every house," Tecumseh had said. Between December 1811 and February 1812, four earthquakes of apocalyptic magnitude, the most intense recorded to date in the history of the region, shook the Mississippi Valley, causing devastation and death. They were felt from the Great Lakes to Florida, which was then under Spanish control, an area greater than three million square kilometers (approximately one million square miles). The effects were so awe-inspiring that the Mississippi River ran backward for a few hours.

The Creek War was a consequence of Tecumseh's call, the inexorable expansion of the United States, internal disagreements between the Creeks that led to a civil war between the Creek factions, and the interference of European powers (namely, Spain, France, and Great Britain), which were interested in supporting the Native Americans to stop the advancement of the United States. When a group of Creeks was ambushed by 180 militiamen in the forest while they were having a noonday meal by the river in July of 1813, the Creeks' radical wing considered it to be a declaration of war. Although they won that first battle, they sought further revenge when they attacked Fort Mims a few weeks later, located in modern Alabama, and massacred 250 defenders and other Native American allies, including civilians, women, and children. The massacre was so abhorrent—the accounts talk of unspeakable cruelty and sadism—that upon hearing the news, the white population became greatly incensed. An American fighter who arrived at the fort after the massacre described the horrific scene he stumbled upon: "Indians, negroes, white men, women and children lay in one promiscuous ruin. All were scalped, and the females of every age were butchered in a manner which neither decency nor language will permit me to describe. The main building was burned to ashes, which were filled with bones. The plains and woods were covered with dead bodies."

Davy heard about the carnage and felt compelled to go. "When I heard of the mischief which was done at the fort, I instantly felt like going, and I had none of the dread of dying that I expected to feel." But Polly was not so convinced. The Crocketts were living in a region where they had no friends or family, and to Polly, the prospect of becoming a widow with three children seemed terrifying. Even so, Davy gathered volunteers and announced that he would go to defend his land and their families. Polly cried a little and then went back to work. "I took a parting farewell of my wife and my little boys, mounted on my horse and set sail to join my company." At the forefront of Tennessee's 5,000 troops was General Andrew Jackson, with whom Davy would cross paths for the first time and whom in a few years would become the seventh president of the United States.

Several days into their journey into the Mississippi Territory, Davy had his first participation in the war. Two men were required to go into the Creek territory on a scouting mission. Since Davy was one of the best shooters, he was chosen to go, and he brought a small band with him. The team crossed the Tennessee River into a hostile region. They advanced thirty miles and found several houses and farms of frightened settlers. The inhabitants knew that if they were seen with the scouts, the Creeks would kill them all. When Davy and his group received reliable reports that the Creeks were marching toward their camp, they made the dangerous journey back under cover of darkness. As they passed through the region, they noticed that everyone had fled and abandoned their homes. When they arrived at the camp, an uninterested colonel dismissed David without uttering a word. Crockett was furious. After all the risks he had taken, to be simply pushed aside like this! When another man in the military, Major John H. Gibson, returned and reported the same thing, the colonel went on alert and mobilized the troops. This, wrote David, "convinced me, clearly, of one of the hateful ways of the world. When I made my report, it wasn't believed, because I was no officer; I was no great man, but just a poor soldier. But when the same thing was reported by Major Gibson why, then, it was all as true as preaching."

Although David spent most of the campaign as a scout and hunter, getting fresh meat for his companions when winter interrupted the supply line, he was involved in some incidents that, despite his belief in the need for war, left a deep mark on his heart. During the attack on the village of Tallushatchee, he wrote:

We shot them like dogs; and then set the house on fire, and burned it up with the forty-six warriors in it. I recollect seeing a boy who was shot down near the house. His arm and thigh were broken, and he was so near the burning house that the grease was stewing out of him. In this situation he was still trying to crawl along; but not a murmur escaped him, though he was only about twelve years old. So sullen is the Indian, when his dander is up, that he had sooner die than make a noise, or ask for quarters.

Davy returned home in time for Christmas to see Polly, his two boys, and a newborn baby girl, but he left them again in January. In the Creek War, future President Andrew Jackson nearly died at the hands of a Native American warrior who had him under his ax when he was saved at the last minute by a Cherokee Indian and ally named Gulkalaski, later renamed Tsunu'lahun'ski. Later, Gulkalaski would regret saving Jackson's life. The Battle of Horseshoe Bend was a devastating defeat for the Native Americans, and with that defeat, the war came to an end, resulting in the loss of 23 million acres of Creek territory, which became the property of the United States as spoils of war. This brought not only the Creek nation to an end but also many other peoples, and the dream of a great Native American federation west of the Mississippi was lost. Crockett returned home to Polly, but if he had hoped to rebuild his family and enjoy the bliss of domestic life, a bitter surprise awaited him.

In 1815, Polly fell seriously ill, and after a few miserable days for the family, she expired in her bed. Crockett was left a widower with three children, one of them a girl who was just a few months old. Feeling like the most miserable man in the world and unsure of what to do with three children, Davy asked his brother and sister-in-law to live with him to lend a hand. However, the presence of these relatives was not the same as genuine maternal care, and David soon realized that he needed to build a new family. That same year, he met Elizabeth Patton, a neighbor who was a war widow and who had been left alone with a daughter and a son. Davy reflected, "I began to think that, as we were both in the same situation, it might be that we could do something for each other." He married Elizabeth soon after.

Historian Michael Wallis recounts a strange occurrence in the ceremony that shows that even in the most solemn of occasions, David´s life was never lacking in adventure and color. When the bride was walking toward the altar, a pig busted through the chapel door, provoking much excitement, laughter, and probably some faintings among the women. The groom kicked the pig out of the chapel, shouting, "Old hook, from now on, I'll do the grunting around here." Crockett perhaps never killed a bear with a single blow of his knife, but he sure could kick a pig out of a church.

Chapter 3 – The Congressman

"Two years ago the inhabitants of this district of which Memphis is the capital sent to the House of Representatives in Congress an individual named David Crockett, who had received no education, could read only with difficulty, had no property, no fixed dwelling, but spent his time hunting, selling his game for a living, and spending his whole life in the woods. "

–Alexis de Tocqueville

"I would sooner be honestly and politically damned, than hypocritically immortalized."

–Davy Crockett

Davy Crockett's political career began in 1821 when he was elected to occupy a seat in the Tennessee General Assembly, his first major public assignment. It was there that he began to demonstrate his skills as a speaker. Six years later, he successfully ran for a seat in the US House of Representatives, where he showed his independent spirit and generosity. At least for the time being, his life as an adventurer and hunter in the woods gave way to another, more civic activity.

After successfully campaigning for a place in the House of Representatives, Crockett sat down to have several portraits of him made, the only images we have of the man since photography did not exist yet. A recently discovered charcoal portrait shows him as a respectable white man in his late twenties or early thirties, with a dark frock coat and a high collar, long sideburns, prominent nose, thin eyebrows, and a plump face. His expression is that of curiosity. However, Crockett's iconography (seven portraits were made in his life) does not fully capture the personality of the hunter, explorer, politician, and hero of Texas of the stories and anecdotes passed down throughout the years. In the paintings, even those made in his lifetime, Crockett looks serious and solemn. His biographers and the contemporary accounts that have survived give a different idea. Crockett was apparently a kind and good-natured person, a wisecracker, and a likable character with a great sense of humor. He always had a fun anecdote ready for any occasion. Generous and simple, even in his days as a congressman, Crockett was always ready to offer what little he had, as he had no attachment to comforts and privileges. He could make a crowd laugh, and his remarks were so ingenious that many people went to the deliberations of Congress to see Davy in action. "It mattered not that Crockett was ignorant of the important questions discussed, and that it was beyond his power to comprehend many of the important measures likely to come before Congress," wrote Edward S. Ellis in a biography he wrote a few years after Davy´s death. "The people felt he was one of them. They took personal pride in his skill with the rifle, and his inimitable powers as a humorist and funny storyteller."

Crockett first served as a representative between 1827 and 1829. In the last year, his old acquaintance Andrew Jackson became president of the United States. During his three terms in Washington, Davy lived in a boarding house in the city and became a recognizable and even an off-the-wall figure in the nation's capital.

Despite his innate generosity, Crockett was not wasteful with public resources. On the contrary, from the little that we know about his interventions, Crockett showed a tendency to limit the power of the government, was against putting more resources in its hands, and refused to use federal money for "charitable works." In a famous incident, Congress proposed to give a pension to the widow of a veteran of the War of 1812. But the man had not died in battle; instead, he had lived many years after the end of the war. Crockett was against that endowment. He asked his fellow congressmen to read the constitution and see how it did not say that Congress could give taxpayer money for charity. "We have the right, as individuals, to give away as much of our own money as we please in charity; but as members of Congress we have no right so to appropriate a dollar of the public money." He added that there were thousands of widows in the country about whom nothing was known. However, this does not mean that David had a cold heart. Immediately afterward, he offered to pay a week of his own salary to the widow, despite the fact that he was "the poorest man on this floor," and he invited all the other congressmen to do the same. In the end, a higher amount than the one originally proposed was collected for the widow.

The frontiersman-become-congressman knew firsthand about the hardships of the common people, those who didn't have the luxuries of Washington, DC. On one occasion, he observed, "I am, sir, but a farmer, destitute of those advantages of education which others possess. I thank heaven I know their worth from having experienced the want of them. The rich require but little legislation. We should at least occasionally legislate for the poor!"

Davy demonstrated that he had an independent spirit and that his commitment to what was right was above his loyalty to President Jackson. "During my two first sessions in Congress, Mr. Adams was president, and I worked along with what was called the Jackson party pretty well," he explained. "I was re-elected to Congress in 1829, by an overwhelming majority; and soon after the commencement of this second term, I saw, or thought I did, that it was expected of me that I would bow to the name of Andrew Jackson, and follow him in all his motions, and windings, and turnings, even at the expense of my conscience and judgment. Such a thing was new to me, and a total stranger to my principles."

His final break with the president was on the occasion of the infamous Indian Removal Act, where Davy gambled his political future. The whole affair possibly contributed to his fatigue with politics.

The Trail of Tears

In his second annual presidential message to Congress in 1830, Andrew Jackson said with satisfaction, "It gives me pleasure to announce to Congress that the benevolent policy of the Government, steadily pursued for nearly thirty years, in relation to the removal of the Indians beyond the white settlements is approaching to a happy consummation." Seven months earlier, Congress had passed, with just three votes of difference, the Indian Removal Act, whereby the Native American tribes still living east of the Mississippi were to renounce all their lands and be relocated to another territory. The law assigned funds and powers to the United States government for the forced removal of the Cherokee and other Native American groups if they objected. The law had been hotly debated during the months of April and May in the Senate and later in the House of Representatives. Davy Crockett opposed it with all of his might.

Although the exodus of tribes to the west of the Mississippi, an operation as aggressive and destructive as those applied to the vanquished in the ancient wars of extermination, is today remembered as one of the darkest incidents of the young American nation, various justifications were offered at the time, mainly the development of agriculture caused an urgent need to incorporate more land. President Jackson also foresaw the need to separate the Native Americans from the white population because he knew that there would be infinite conflicts, and finally, there was the question of interference from other countries. At a time when the final borders of the United States had not yet been defined (the entire west belonged to Mexico), Spain and France made secret alliances with the tribes to make war on the US. All of these justifications, in one way or another, were a part of Manifest Destiny, the philosophy that saw westward expansion as a divine mandate for moral progress and the expansion of Christianity and civilization at the hands of God's people: the United States.

In a letter sent to the official US interpreter at the Choctaw Agency, John Pitchlynn, in 1830, the president, who had referred to the tribes as barbarians with "savage habits," asked him to communicate to the Native Americans:

> Their happiness, peace & prosperity depends upon their removal beyond the jurisdiction of the laws of the State of Mississippi. These things have been [often times] explained to them fully and I forbear to repeat them; but request that you make known to them that Congress to enable them to remove & comfortably to arrange themselves at their new homes has made liberal appropriations. It was a measure I had much at heart & sought to effect because I was satisfied that the Indians could not possibly live under the laws of the States. If now they shall refuse to accept the liberal terms offered, they only must be liable for whatever evils & difficulties may arise. I feel conscious of having done my duty to my red children and if any failure of my good intention arises, it will be attributable to their want of duty to themselves, not to me.

But in the end, it was just Jackson's nonsensical way to dress up what they were doing. The reality was simple and crude: the tribes did not want to give up their lands, and the act was a humiliating dispossession, no matter how much the president tried to embellish it with good intentions.

Many congressmen strongly opposed the law. Crockett had experienced firsthand the rigors of warring against the Indians, as he had participated in the attack on Tallushatchee, but he understood that beneath all that talk was a strong nation acting unkindly against weaker ones. He understood that if it was carried out, the Indian Removal Act would be remembered as one of the most shameful events in the history of the nation. Congressman Crockett was one of the few whites who dared to openly oppose the presidential initiative, and he was the only one from Tennessee to do so. According to the Congressional Register of Debates, Crockett said that he knew many of the Chickasaw tribe because they lived near his district and that he would not consent to move them against their will to an unknown land where the United States had no property. He also said that he knew that the Cherokees would rather die than leave their home, and he repeated their words: "No, we will take death here at our homes. Let them come and tomahawk us here at home: we are willing to die."

In doing so, Crockett became not only Jackson's enemy but also one to the Tennessee voters, who craved more Native American territory to turn into farmland. Crockett preferred to follow the dictates of his conscience. "I opposed it from the purest motives in the world," he wrote in his autobiography. "Several of my colleagues told me how I was ruining myself. They said this was a favourite measure of the president, and I ought to go for it. I told them I believed it was a wicked, unjust measure, and that I should go against it, let the cost to myself be what it might; that I was willing to go with General Jackson in every thing that I believed was honest and right. I voted against this Indian bill, and my conscience yet tells me that I gave a good honest vote, and one that I believe will not make me ashamed in the day of judgment."

The strongly enforced Indian Removal Act is one of the most controversial acts not only in Andrew Jackson´s presidency but in the history of the United States, to the degree that some commentators have called it genocide. It set a sad precedent for what would be the rest of the expansion toward the Pacific, marked by the idea that the Americans were the chosen people who were called to possess all of North America. When the Indian Removal Act was carried out, the tribes were, for the most part, brought against their will into the current state of Oklahoma.

The exodus that took place at the point of bayonets is known as the Trail of Tears. The Native Americans suffered unspeakable hardships and left many dead on the journey. Hundreds died from starvation and from exposure to the elements. "My heart bleeds when I reflect on his cruelty to the poor Indians. I never expected it of him [Jackson]," lamented Crockett. Tsunu'lahun'ski, the Cherokee veteran of the Creek War who had saved Jackson's life, said, "If I had known that Jackson would drive us from our homes, I would have killed him at Horseshoe." To date, many Native Americans refuse to touch twenty-dollar bills, as it has the portrait of Andrew Jackson on it.

Crockett's brave stance earned him the recognition of the Native American nations. Cherokee Chief John Ross wrote him a letter in which he said that Davy´s vote in Congress had "and will produce for you among the friends of humanity & justice a just respect and admiration." In turn, Crockett was always proud to say that he did not obey any master or political party. "Look at my neck, and you will not find there a necklace with the engraving: [this is] MY DOG - ANDREW JACKSON," he wrote shortly after winning his first reelection as a congressman.

Still, that was perhaps the beginning of the end of his political career. Opposing Jackson, who was just beginning his eight-year stay in office, was not a clever move, much less in Tennessee. "Jackson was ill-tempered, a fierce hater, unbending, dictatorial and vindictive," writes Mel Ayton, an author of American history and true crime books. His opponents placed many traps for Crockett, like scheduling a tour of Tennessee for him, where he would have to explain to many angry voters why he had sided with the Cherokee. The press also destroyed him, accusing him of being a player, a charlatan, a trickster, and a drunk. Another newspaper made fun of the stories told about him regarding his adventures in the woods. For his part, Jackson commented on Davy Crockett's reelection campaign, saying, "I trust, for the honor of the state, your Congressional District will not disgrace themselves longer by sending that profligate man Crockett back to Congress."

Frustrated by the multitude of attacks, especially the lies of his adversary in the congressional reelection campaign, a 34-year-old lawyer named William Fitzgerald, Crockett publicly threatened to beat him up if he insulted him again. When the two men met at a public event in Tennessee, Fitzgerald took the stand and placed an object on the table covered with a cloth. When Fitzgerald began slandering Crockett as he stared at him, Davy got up and ran to his opponent, ready to pulverize him. It was a naive act and his biggest political mistake. Fast as lightning, Fitzgerald pulled out a pistol that was hidden under the cloth and aimed it at Crockett's chest, warning him that if he took another step, it would be his end. Confounded by the unexpected action, David froze and returned to his seat, stunned.

Crockett said goodbye to politics as only he could. "You may all go to hell; I will go to Texas," he told his constituents at the end of his last term in 1835, for he had decided that exploring and crossing new borders was more fun than living in a boarding house near the Capitol. And he was only on his way to becoming a legend.

Chapter 4 – The Celebrity

"Him an' his jokes travelled all through the land
an' his speeches made him friends to beat the band,
his politickin' was their favorite brand
an' everyone wanted to shake his hand."
—*The Ballad of Davy Crockett*, 1955

It is a characteristic of free-spirited people, like Davy Crockett, to have a rebellious and indomitable side that is not always well regarded by society. After passing through Congress, Crockett sold his property and rented a piece of forest, where he set out to build a cabin, sow the land, and plant fruit trees. But Elizabeth, his second wife, could not cope anymore with the "bad" behavior of her husband, which the newspapers called vices. So, they may not have been all an invention of the press. The famous hunter and frontiersman constantly abandoned his family to go on expeditions, and he had a problem with drinking—something that was common in this period in America. His wife left him, and suddenly, David found himself without a political career or a marriage. Throughout the year of 1832, he lived alone in his cabin and passed the days hunting bears, while the exaggerated tales of his exploits continued to grow. The newspapers, aware that their readers wanted more frontier adventures, did not shy away from delivering and even inventing more wild tales.

In 1831, a play by James Kirke Paulding, called *The Lion of the West*, featured a man named Colonel Nimrod Wildfire, who was a caricature of Crockett. Although the play did not bear his name, people recognized that it was a tribute to the hunter. An assistant recalled how, when the play was about to begin, Crockett appeared at the entrance and was escorted by the manager to the first row, where they had a seat reserved for him. The audience erupted in applause. When the curtain was lifted, and the actor appeared with his raccoon cap, impersonating the royal frontiersman in the front row, David rose again from his seat and bowed toward the audience.

The play´s character imitated Davy's colorful way of speaking. It is difficult to know whether Crockett actually said many of the things that are attributed to him or if they were taken from plays, fake news, and almanacs. But one of Crockett's most esteemed phrases is undeniably authentic: "Be always sure you are right, then go ahead." However, the context in which this maxim first appears is not romantic or heroic by today's standards: the frontiersman scribbled it on a contract for the sale of a black slave named Adaline, for the sum of $300, whom he was forced to sell to pay his eternal debt. It is worth mentioning that Crockett, like many other families of Tennessee, didn't own many slaves, and there was even an anti-slavery sentiment in the region. According to the 1820 census, there was only one slave in the Crockett household.

At a popular level, however, the common people made Crockett's alleged exploits reach mythical proportions. It was said that he was going to jump and ride the tail of Halley's Comet, which appeared on the horizon in 1835. Davy himself, with his strong personality, his exploits, and autobiographical books, the first of which was published in 1834, fueled Crockett-mania.

A note in Boston's *Daily Evening Transcript*, after Crockett's visit to Washington, reported a fantastic incident, which serves as proof that the newspapers of the time not only indulged in many poetic licenses but also of the mythical character of Crockett, who was a kind of prototype of America's superhero. The *Daily Evening Transcript* says that during Crockett's first visit to the country's capital in 1828, a caravan of wild animals was in an exhibition in the city. Large crowds were gaping before the beasts, and the famous frontiersman was there too. "The house was very much crowded," Crockett says in this highly fictionalized account.

The first thing I noticed was two wildcats in a cage. Some acquaintances asked me if they were like the wildcats in the backwoods, and as I was looking at them, one turned over and died. The keeper ran up and threw some water on it. Said hi, stranger you are wasting time. My looks kill them things, and you had better hire me to go out there or I will kill every varmint you´ve got.

In addition to his very real adventures in the woods, Davy allowed and exploited these fairy tales and the tendency of the people to mythologize him, a trend that continued after his death until he became a kind of demi-god, a cycle that is studied today by anthropologists interested in myth formation in North America. Davy Crockett's real and fictional feats were exploited by the Whig Party, one of the two great political parties in the first half of the 19th century in the United States. His extraordinary tales deal with the themes of the self-made American man and the myth of the almost supernatural but still mortal hero, who finds his death through a treacherous act or is unnaturally slain.

Not that Crockett was alien to adventures or heroic deeds, even before his participation in the Battle of the Alamo. In 1835, when President Jackson was leaving a funeral in the Capitol building, an unemployed painter approached him and said, "I'll be damned if I don't do it," drew his gun, and shot the president. The man had a terrible aim. Jackson, an old soldier, tried to defend himself with his stick. The unemployed painter pulled a second pistol from his clothes and shot the 67-year-old president again, only to fail a second time. "I know where this came from," shouted Jackson, thinking that the Whigs had sent the madman to kill him. Davy was close to Jackson and ran, along with Navy Lieutenant Thomas Gedney, to seize the would-be assassin and then rushed the president to a carriage. The unemployed painter spent the rest of his life in a mental asylum.

When Crockett had enough of this mythification, he decided to disappear and escape from hell, like Orpheus, although it was not the real underworld that Crockett escaped from but rather Washington politics and the Mississippi Valley. In search of new frontiers, Crockett said goodbye to his constituents in his inimitable style. "Since you have chosen to elect a man with a timber toe to succeed me, you may all go to hell and I will go to Texas." In this way, the legendary frontiersman prepared to cross a new border, this time that of his own country.

Chapter 5 – Gone to Texas: The Freedom Fighter

"Do not be uneasy about me, I am with my friends."
—Davy Crockett's last known letter, January 1836

For a time, it was common to see these three letters roughly drawn with a knife on the doors of Tennessee houses: GTT. The initials meant that the aforementioned had taken his few belongings and left for Texas in search of a new beginning. Like many other people who had lost everything or were fleeing the law, Davy Crockett, with a finished political career, a broken family, an absent wife, and with no place to call home, fulfilled his promise of going to Texas and Mexico instead of staying in a country where his adversaries made everything increasingly difficult. Texas was offering more than 4,000 acres to each person who came to colonize it. Davy's intention was to explore that piece of northern Mexico and try to make "a fortune" for his family. Along with a small group of people, including his nephew, his brother-in-law, and a neighbor, he made the long trip from Tennessee to Texas under the ghostly light of Halley's Comet, which, in those months, was visible at night. When he crossed the Red River, he was effectively saying goodbye to the United States and entering another country. "I do believe Santa Anna's kingdom [Mexico] will be a paradise compared with this [the United States under Jackson]."

In January 1836, he wrote to his daughter, saying, "I must say as to what I have seen of Texas it is the garden spot of the world the best land and best prospect for health I ever saw is here and I do believe it is a fortune to any man to come here." Crockett was enthusiastic, and according to the people who saw him, he was almost euphoric with the new life that awaited him since he was certain that he would finally get some good land. "I have no doubt that it is the richest country in the world," he wrote in a letter, without using commas or other punctuation marks. "Good land and plenty of timber and the best springs and good millstreams good range clear water it is in the pass where the buffalo passes from north to south twice a year and bees and honey plenty."

Davy was about to turn fifty. Although in our day, fifty is considered to be relatively young, in the early 19th century, a man of that age was already in his golden years. So, when Davy Crockett participated in the Battle of the Alamo, he was officially an elderly person, far from the images that are known of him as a young man in his twenties, full of vitality, with a raccoon cap on his head, knocking down ten Mexican soldiers with a single blow. All in all, despite being in his sixth decade of life, Davy remained in very good shape thanks to the active life he had led. Wars, hunting, and scouting had hardened him. Politics was apparently the only thing that had left him exhausted.

Mexican *Tejas*

The Americans called it Texas, but its official name was the "New Kingdom of Philippines, Province of Tejas." It was a part of Mexico, although the name "New Kingdom of Philippines" was already in disuse, and the Mexican government simply called it *Tejas*. For centuries, the territory had been largely uninhabited by Europeans. At the beginning of the 19th century, the total population did not exceed 3,500 Mexicans, who lived in the towns of San Antonio de Béxar (modern San Antonio) and Bahía del Espíritu Santo (modern

Goliad). Since Mexico's independence in 1810, the government had been concerned with this unoccupied and yet so promising part of the country.

In 1820, the Mexican government had begun an active colonization policy for Texas to check the Apache incursions. The government gave away the land and granted tax exemptions and the free import of necessary items for the new colony. They were such exceptional conditions that US Secretary of State Henry Clay could not help but exclaim, "Mexicans must have little interest in keeping Texas, since they are giving it away!" However, hardly anyone in Mexico wanted to move north because Texas was the region of the Apache, the Comanche, Cherokee, and other relentless warrior tribes.

One of the persons who took the offer was an American named Moses Austin, who began to organize the transfer of 300 families to the region. Old Austin died before taking the road, and it fell upon his son, Stephen Austin, to take the Old Three Hundred on that journey. Stephen appeared in the city of San Antonio in August 1821 before the governor of Texas, Antonio Martínez, who gave him permission to explore the land and find a suitable place to establish a colony. Accompanied by some Native American friends and guides, Austin made his way to the Gulf Coast and built a settlement. In 1826, he presided over 1,800 people, of whom about a quarter were black slaves.

The newcomers had a clear sense of identity. Compared to the Mexicans who lived in Texas, the Anglos were more educated, they were better off economically, and they were Protestants with a capitalistic spirit and highly driven by their personal freedoms. This was of paramount importance to unite them around a common cause. In 1830, the so-called *Texians*, the Anglo settlers, tripled the Mexican *Tejanos*. Many Americans from the Mississippi area, who were affected by the agricultural crisis and fleeing from debtors, began arriving en masse with their slaves. The problem was that Mexico had abolished slavery in 1830 by order of the first president of African ancestry in the Americas, Vicente Guerrero. Although President

Guerrero temporarily exempted Texas from the law, the news shook the settlers since almost all of them had slaves. Andrew Jackson offered Mexico five million dollars in exchange for Texas. The proposal could not have come at a worse time for the alarmed Mexican authorities, though, as they were watching the territory slip from their hands. Many lands north of the Nueces River were sold to speculators in New York, although they were occupied by Mexicans and Native Americans.

In 1835, a major change occurred in Mexico that fueled the cause of independence in Texas. In that year, a new constitution put an end to federalism and inaugurated a centralist system, under which states lost their power, thus creating what is known to historians as the Central Republic of Mexico. Under the new regime, the authority resided in the country's capital, limits were placed on who could vote, and sovereign states were abrogated and replaced with departments. Meanwhile, *Tejas* had become Texas—the Anglo population had grown to 35,000 people. Most of them had entered illegally, but there was no denying the fact that the de facto language in the province was English and that the Hispanic population was being expelled across the Nueces River.

In September 1835, when the new Central Republic came into effect, the Texas settlers disavowed the Mexican government. Up to this point, their intention was apparently to rebel against the centralist regime and return to the Mexican Republic once federalism was restored. Austin was officially in command of the movement, but he had no military experience. Within weeks, most of his men deserted and returned to their fields. A personal friend of President Jackson, Sam Houston, arrived in Texas and took the command from Austin, leading 300 men from New Orleans and Mississippi. Throughout the United States, Houston presented Texas as the promised land where everyone could get rich as long as they brought a rifle to help. In December, the pro-independence rebels seized the Alamo fort—an old Franciscan mission built by the Spanish—which was guarded by a party of malnourished Mexican guards, who had arrived in San

Antonio tied by their necks in order to prevent them from fleeing. By March 1836, there was not a single Mexican soldier left in Texas.

The President of Mexico, Antonio López de Santa Anna, went berserk when he heard the news. In February 1836, he marched north with 6,000 men to subdue the Texas rebels. On February 23rd, the Mexican troops arrived at the Alamo. Davy Crockett was inside.

How Did Crockett Arrive at the Alamo?

How in the world did Davy Crockett end up inside a fort surrounded by Santa Anna's army? For this, we have to go back a few months, when he crossed the Red River into the Mexican province of Texas, where tensions with the federal government of Mexico were about to erupt. David spent his first days making stops at different farms, where people lodged him. He hunted and explored, looking for a place to settle. He spent the winter looking for buffalo and other game. On one occasion, when he did not return in time to celebrate Christmas with her guests, the family feared the worst, and word spread that Davy Crockett had died at the hands of the Native Americans. Several newspapers reported his passing, but as always, the mythical man defeated death and reappeared with the best of spirits to move on. As he made his way south, word spread that the famous frontiersman, the one who could shoot the moon and kill a bear with a single stab, was entering Austin´s land. Crockett's fame as an adventurer and uncanny explorer was greater than as a politician. Rumors that he was going to join the cause of Texas independence were received by the colonists as if Achilles *redivivus* had come to fight Santa Anna.

Crockett arrived in excellent spirits at Nacogdoches in January 1836 with other men who had joined his caravan, attracted by the promise of cheap lands and the opportunity to make a fortune. Crockett was welcomed with enthusiasm, and they offered him a banquet. He received adoration from the people when he uttered his famous phrase where he said that he had left hell to go to what must logically be the kingdom of heaven: "I was, for some years, a member of Congress. In my last canvass, I told the people of my district that if they saw fit to reelect me, I would serve them as faithfully as I had done before. But, if not, they might go to hell and I would go to Texas. I was beaten, gentlemen, and here I am."

Several revolutionaries were concentrated in Nacogdoches, the oldest town in Texas, where the Spaniards had built a mission in 1716. In this town, Crockett understood that if he aspired to receive land and to have a position in the government of the new republic, he would have to sign an oath of allegiance to the government of the, until then hypothetical, Republic of Texas, and more importantly, he would have to take the offer to serve as a mercenary for the rebels. From Nacogdoches, he went to the town of San Augustine, where he wrote his famous last letter to his daughter.

> I have taken the oath of the Government and have enrolled my name as a volunteer for six months and will set out for the Rio Grand in a few days with the volunteers from the United States...all volunteers is entitled to a vote for a member of the convention or to be voted for and I have but little doubt of being elected a member to form a constitution for this province.

On January 16th, 1836, Crockett joined a band of armed men led by a certain Captain William Harrison. Although Davy was a common foot soldier, he was the center of attention. The mythical Davy Crockett was walking among them! On his way south, he took the opportunity to demonstrate his hunting skills to get food for the soldiers, as he had done in his youth during the Creek War, until they arrived at Sam Houston's headquarters in Washington-on-the-Brazos. From there, Davy left for San Antonio. Along the way, he stopped at John Swisher's farm, who left an invaluable description of Crockett's physical appearance: "I judged him to be about forty years old. He was stout and muscular, about six feet in height, and weighing 180 to 200 pounds. He was of a florid complexion, with intelligent gray eyes. He had small side whiskers, inclining to sandy. He was fond of talking and had an ease and grace about him."

In February, after several days of enjoying the hospitality of the Swisher family, Crockett headed to San Antonio de Béxar. There, he appeared in the plaza and spoke in what already seemed to be a full-fledged political campaign: "Fellow citizens, I am among you. I have come to your country, though not I hope, through any selfish motive whatever. I have come to aid you all that I can in your noble cause." From there, he marched to the Alamo with a dozen men. The men at the Alamo, who were ecstatic at seeing Crockett, demanded a speech from the legendary man. His presence was felt as if the savior himself had descended from the clouds, especially at the news that Santa Anna was approaching the fort with his dragoons, as everyone was now expecting a merciless fight. But Crockett was the man who could shoot and hit the moon—the Alamo was in good hands.

The Battle of the Alamo

When Santa Anna's army arrived in the vicinity of San Antonio, there were between 180 and 250 fighters and several frightened citizens inside the Alamo. Santa Anna first sent a white-flagged messenger to offer the defenders a chance to surrender, but before he arrived, William Travis, who was in charge of the fort, shot him. This act angered the Mexicans, who then planted a red flag, meaning they would take no prisoners. Santa Anna subjected the fort to an incessant rain of cannon fire and artillery, gaining ground every day. However, according to some eyewitnesses from San Antonio, "Santa Anna left the East side of the Alamo unprotected, waiting for the *Texians* to leave in peace and save the Mexican army from a costly victory." According to other testimonies, Crockett and his men fought under the flag of Mexico, with the date "1824" stamped on it, which is the year of the signing of the Mexican Constitution. The image of a homogeneous group of Anglo defenders fighting against Mexicans is also fiction, as evidenced by numerous testimonies compiled by historian Timothy Matovina, the director of the Institute for Latino Studies at the University of Notre Dame, Indiana. Both inside and outside the Alamo, many Hispanics fought alongside the Anglo defenders.

On March 5th, the Mexican Army paused the attack, possibly as a psychological tactic, as the defenders of the fort were caught asleep in the early hours of the 6th. After a fierce battle, lasting an hour and a half, the clash ended in furious hand-to-hand combat, a moment that has passed into the history of Texas as one of its most heroic episodes. For many years, it was believed that Crockett and his men from Tennessee died defending one of the fortress walls until the end. "Here, am I, Colonel, assign us to some place, and I and my Tennessee boys will defend it all right," Crockett allegedly said, according to a version of the conflict published in 1911. Travis assigned him and his band the duty of protecting the low wall and stockade on the south side of the fort, where they died in a desperate fight. The embellished stories that followed Davy like a shadow reported that dozens of dead Mexican soldiers were found around his pierced body. However, no one ever recovered Crockett's body.

The appearance in the mid-20th century of a lost diary by a Mexican captain named José Enrique de la Peña, who fought at the Alamo with Santa Anna, put to rest all the glorious descriptions of Davy Crockett´s last moments. According to de la Peña's testimony, Crockett did not die inside the Alamo. He and a small group fought to the end until they were captured and brought alive to Santa Anna. The diary's discovery produced a wave of outrage and skepticism, with allegations that the document was a forgery. But José de la Peña left not only a description of Crockett's ultimate fate that other sources have since confirmed but also a beautiful portrait of the man in his last moments.

Some seven men had survived the general carnage and, under the protection of general Castrillón, they were brought before Santa Anna. Among them was one of great stature well proportioned with regular features, in whose face there was the imprint of adversity but in whom one also noticed a degree of resignation and nobility that did him honor. He was the naturalist David Crockett, well known in North America for his unusual adventures, who had undertaken to explore the country and who, finding himself in Béjar [San Antonio] at the very moment of surprise, had taken refuge in the Alamo fearing that his status as a foreigner might not be respected. Santa Anna answered Castrillón's intervention in Crockett´s behalf with a gesture of indignation and, addressing himself to...the troops closest to him, ordered his execution.

De la Peña expresses horror and shame at what happened next. According to his testimony, the commanders were outraged at this order and did not support it, hoping that Santa Anna would cool down once the fury of the moment had passed. But the president's personal guard, wanting to win his favor, slaughtered the prisoners with their swords right on the spot. Davy thus crossed a final and definitive frontier, one from which there would be no return. "I turned away horrified in order not to witness such a barbarous scene," wrote de la Peña. He notes one last act of Crockett´s nobility, saying, "Though tortured before they were killed, these unfortunates died without complaining and without humiliating themselves before their torturers."

The revelation that Davy did not die at the Alamo should not have come as a surprise. The scene matches Edward Ellis's description in his biography published in 1884, though Ellis adds that Crockett resisted.

At last only six of the garrison were left alive. They were surrounded by General Castrillon and his soldiers. The officer shouted to them to surrender, promising that their lives should be spared. In the little group of Spartans were Davy Crockett and Travis, so exhausted they were scarcely able to stand. Crockett stood in an angle of the fort, the barrel of his shattered rifle in his right hand, while the massive Bowie in his left was dripping with blood. His face was crimson from a gash in his forehead, and nearly a score of Mexicans were stretched around him, either dead or dying from his fearful blows. There were a few brave and humane officers, and among them were General Castrillon and Burdillon. They spoke sympathizingly to Crockett and Travis, and with several other officers walked to where the scowling Santa Anna stood and asked that the surrender of the few survivors might be received. The reply was an order that all should be shot. Seeing his treachery, the enraged Crockett roused himself, and swinging his Bowie aloft, made a furious rush for the Mexican Nana Sahib. The intrepid Tennessean was riddled with bullets before he could pass half the intervening distance.

In the end, it doesn't matter if the hero died inside or outside the Alamo, shooting his rifle or with his hands tied, or even how many Mexicans he killed. The fact is that Davy Crockett shared the fate of his companions and that he was ready to give up his life for a cause that he considered to be just. After the unfortunate incident, all of the Alamo's dead were stripped of their clothes, cut to pieces, and piled on top of each other. Then they were incinerated, a particularly humiliating fate for the deceased at the time. The ashes of the defenders remained there for more than a year until a party arrived to put them inside a chest in March 1837, after which they buried them in a nearby site, which has not been found to this day.

Chapter 6 – The Myth

"Davy Crockett could run faster than any man in Tennessee. He could stare down a streak of lightning without blinking. He could pull a rainbow out of the sky. He had the surest rifle and the ugliest dog anywhere."

—20th-century popular book about Davy Crockett

When he was alive, fame embraced Davy Crockett. After his death, it grew to unsuspected heights. Davy Crockett's first almanacs— a type of yearbook that was very popular until the mid-20th century that was directed primarily at peasants with information on harvests, the phases of the moon, and other meteorological phenomena—appeared in Nashville in 1835 and 1836, which was during Crockett's lifetime. They continued to appear for years afterward. In addition to the usual information, Davy Crockett´s almanacs told anecdotes of his life, to which the American public had become addicted. Almost all of them bordered on exaggerations and myths. Some of them may have been reworkings of stories that the frontiersman himself told his friends. He allegedly fought a cougar and won. Another story said that, on one occasion, he sighted a wild stallion on the prairie. When he was within a few steps of the horse, it came snorting at him, but Crockett jumped and mounted it. The horse started to run like lightning and ran for three days, with its rider holding its mane, until they came to a "Mad

River." There, the horse ran under a tree, trying to brush Crockett off its back, but the brave man leaped over the tree, and the horse finally stopped, allowing Crockett to get off.

In other tales, Davy is like a character of ancient myths, making huge leaps that transported him over long distances and even among the planets. His popularity was revived in the 1950s with a Disney movie that introduced an almost forgotten Crockett to a generation that had never heard of him, especially children, with a refurbished image, juvenile looks, and his classic raccoon cap. He was the king of the wild frontier, a man who fixed the crack in the Liberty Bell and fixed up the government. Reacting to his incredible surge in popularity, *Harper's Magazine* retorted in a cynical editorial that Crockett was never "a king of anything except maybe the Tennessee Tall Tales and Bourbon Samplers Association."

For Texans, he is an untouchable figure; for baby boomers, a beloved figure of their childhood; for his country, a brave and honest congressman; and for the Native American nations, an honorable enemy and later a compassionate human being. Crockett was, after all, a man who always acted chivalrously, sometimes perhaps a little too idealistic. He was a man with strong convictions that had been ingrained in a life lived on the border, not only a physical border but a social one as well. His temperament made him face adversaries—natural and human—bigger and more powerful than he: the border, wild beasts, the president of the USA, a foreign army. Davy Crockett always took the challenges that were presented to him with a resolution worthy of admiration, with a heart that didn't know hypocrisy.

His death in the Battle of the Alamo got him a ticket to the pantheon of heroes, but Davy would probably be the first one to frown upon that idea. "Most men are remembered as they died, and not as they lived," he wrote in 1834. "We gaze with admiration upon the glories of the setting sun, yet scarcely bestow a passing glance upon its noonday splendor. I know not whether, in the eyes of the world, a brilliant death is not preferred to an obscure life of rectitude." And in the case of Davy Crockett, it will always be his life and the ideals that he defended when he was alive that will grant him a place among the great men of America.

References

Blackburn, Thomas. *The Ballad of Davy Crockett.* (Recorded by Fess Parker). Columbia Records, 1955.

Christensen, Carol and Thomas. *The US-Mexican War.* USA: Bay Books San

Francisco, 1998.

Crockett, David. *Life of David Crockett, the Original Humorist and Irrepressible Backwoodsman. An Autobiography.* New York: AL Burt, 1902

Ellis, Edward Sylvester. *The Life of Colonel David Crockett.* Philadelphia: Porter & Coates, 1884.

Loomis, C. Grant. "Davy Crockett Visits Boston." *The New England Quarterly,* vol. 20, no. 3, 1947, pp. 396–400.

Matovina, Timothy M. *The Alamo Remembered: Tejano Accounts and*

Perspectives. USA: University of Texas Press, 1995.

Wallis, Michael. *David Crockett, The Lion of the West.* New York: Norton & Company, 2011.

Williams, Amelia. "A Critical Study of the Siege of the Alamo and of the Personnel of Its Defenders: IV. Historical Problems Relating to the Alamo." *The Southwestern Historical Quarterly* 37, no. 3 (1934): 157-84.

Here's another book by Captivating History
that you might be interested in

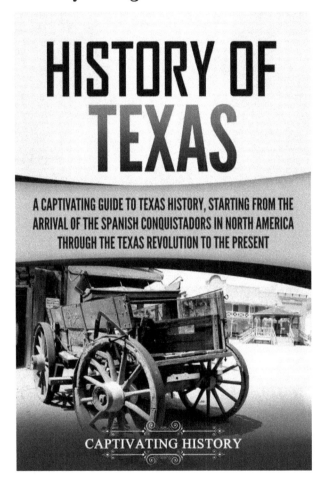